'I POURED SOME VODKA; BRANDO DECLINED TO JOIN ME.'

TRUMAN CAPOTE
Born 1924, New Orleans, Louisiana, USA
Died 1984, Bel-Air, Los Angeles, USA

Truman Capote interviewed Marlon Brando – the Duke –
whilst the Hollywood icon was taking a break from the
filming of *Sayonara* in a hotel room in Kyoto, Japan in 1956.
The Duke in His Domain was first published in the *New Yorker*
in 1957.

CAPOTE IN PENGUIN MODERN CLASSICS
Answered Prayers
Breakfast at Tiffany's
A Capote Reader
The Complete Stories
The Early Stories of Truman Capote
In Cold Blood
Music for Chameleons
My Side of the Matter
Other Voices, Other Rooms
Summer Crossing

TRUMAN CAPOTE

The Duke in His Domain

PENGUIN BOOKS

PENGUIN CLASSICS

UK | USA | Canada | Ireland | Australia
India | New Zealand | South Africa

Penguin Books is part of the Penguin Random House group
of companies whose addresses can be found at
global.penguinrandomhouse.com.

This edition first published 2018
004

Set in 10.25/12.75 pt Dante MT Std
Typeset by Jouve (UK), Milton Keynes
Printed and bound in Great Britain by Clays Ltd, Elcograf S.p.A.

ISBN: 978-0-241-33914-5

www.greenpenguin.co.uk

Most Japanese girls giggle. The little maid on the fourth floor of the Miyako Hotel, in Kyoto, was no exception. Hilarity, and attempts to suppress it, pinked her cheeks (unlike the Chinese, the Japanese complexion more often than not has considerable color), shook her plump peony-and-pansy-kimonoed figure. There seemed to be no particular reason for this merriment; the Japanese giggle operates without apparent motivation. I'd merely asked to be directed toward a certain room. 'You come see Marron?' she gasped, showing, like so many of her fellow-countrymen, an array of gold teeth. Then, with the tiny, pigeon-toed skating steps that the wearing of a kimono necessitates, she led me through a labyrinth of corridors, promising, 'I knock you Marron.' The 'l' sound does not exist in Japanese, and by 'Marron' the maid meant Marlon – Marlon Brando, the American actor, who was at that time in Kyoto doing location work for the Warner Brothers – William Goetz motion-picture version of James Michener's novel *Sayonara*.

My guide tapped at Brando's door, shrieked 'Marron!' and fled away along the corridor, her kimono sleeves fluttering like the wings of a parakeet. The door was opened by another doll-delicate Miyako maid, who at once succumbed to her own fit of quaint hysteria. From an inner room, Brando called, 'What is it, honey?' But the girl, her eyes squeezed shut with mirth and her fat little hands jammed into her mouth, like a bawling baby's, was incapable of reply. 'Hey, honey, what is it?' Brando again inquired, and appeared in the doorway. 'Oh, hi,' he said when he saw me. 'It's seven, huh?' We'd made a seven-o'clock date for dinner; I was nearly twenty minutes late. 'Well, take off your shoes and come on in. I'm just finishing up here. And, hey, honey,' he told the maid, 'bring us some ice.' Then, looking after the girl as she scurried off, he cocked his hands on his hips and, grinning, declared, 'They kill me. They really kill me. The kids, too. Don't you think they're wonderful, don't you love them – Japanese kids?'

The Miyako, where about half of the *Sayonara* company was staying, is the most prominent of the so-called Western-style hotels in Kyoto; the majority of its rooms are furnished with sturdy, if commonplace and cumbersome, European chairs and tables, beds and couches. But for the convenience of Japanese guests, who prefer their own mode of décor while desiring the prestige of staying at the Miyako, or of those foreign travelers who yearn after authentic atmosphere yet are disinclined to endure the unheated rigors of a real Japanese inn, the Miyako maintains some suites decorated in the traditional manner, and it was in one of these that Brando had chosen to settle himself. His quarters consisted of two rooms, a bath and a glassed-in sun porch. Without the overlying and underlying clutter of Brando's personal belongings, the rooms would have been textbook illustrations of the Japanese penchant for an ostentatious barrenness. The floors were covered with tawny *tatami* matting, with a discreet scattering of raw-silk pillows; a scroll depicting swimming golden carp hung in an alcove, and beneath it, on a stand, sat a vase filled with tall lilies and red leaves, arranged just so. The larger of the two rooms – the inner one – which the occupant was using as a sort of business office where he also dined and slept, contained a long, low lacquer table and a sleeping pallet. In these rooms, the divergent concepts of Japanese and Western decoration – the one seeking to impress by a lack of display, an absence of possession-exhibiting, the other intent on precisely the reverse – could both be observed, for Brando seemed unwilling to make use of the apartment's storage space, concealed behind sliding paper doors. All that he owned seemed to be out in the open. Shirts, ready for the laundry; socks, too; shoes and sweaters and jackets and hats and ties, flung around like the costume of a dismantled scarecrow. And cameras, a typewriter, a tape recorder, an electric heater that performed with stifling competence. Here, there, pieces of partly nibbled fruit; a box of the famous Japanese strawberries, each berry the size of an egg. And books, a deep-thought cascade, among which one saw Colin Wilson's *The Outsider* and various works on Buddhist prayer, Zen meditation, Yogi breathing and Hindu mysticism, but no fiction, for Brando reads none. He has never, he professes, opened a novel since April 3, 1924, the day he was born, in Omaha, Nebraska. But while he may not care to read fiction, he does desire to write it, and the long lacquer table was loaded with overfilled ashtrays and piled pages of his most

recent creative effort, which happens to be a film script entitled
A Burst of Vermilion.

In fact, Brando had evidently been working on his story at
the moment of my arrival. As I entered the room, a subdued-
looking, youngish man, whom I shall call Murray, and who
had previously been pointed out to me as 'the fellow that's
helping Marlon with his writing', was squatted on the matting,
fumbling through the manuscript of *A Burst of Vermilion*.
Weighing some pages on his hand, he said, 'Tell ya, Mar, s'pose
I go over this down in my room, and maybe we'll get together
again – say, around ten-thirty?'

Brando scowled, as though unsympathetic to the idea of
resuming their endeavors later in the evening. Having been
slightly ill, as I learned later, he had spent the day in his room,
and now seemed restive. 'What's this?' he asked, pointing to
a couple of oblong packages among the literary remains on
the lacquer table.

Murray shrugged. The maid had delivered them; that was
all he knew. 'People are always sending Mar presents,' he told
me. 'Lots of times we don't know who sent them. True, Mar?'

'Yeah,' said Brando, beginning to rip open the gifts, which,
like most Japanese packages – even mundane purchases from
very ordinary shops – were beautifully wrapped. One contained candy, the other white rice cakes, which proved
cement-hard, though they looked like puffs of cloud. There
was no card in either package to identify the donor. 'Every
time you turn around, some Japanese is giving you a present. They're crazy about giving presents,' Brando observed.

Athletically crunching a rice cake, he passed the boxes to Murray and me.

Murray shook his head, he was intent on obtaining Brando's promise to meet with him again at ten-thirty. 'Give me a ring around then,' Brando said, finally. 'We'll see what's happening.'

Murray, as I knew, was only one member of what some of the *Sayonara* company referred to as 'Brando's gang'. Aside from the literary assistant, the gang consisted of Marlon Brando, Sr., who acts as his son's business manager; a pretty, dark-haired secretary, Miss Levin; and Brando's private make-up man. The travel expenses of this entourage, and all its living expenses while on location, were allowed for in the actor's contract with Warner Brothers. Legend to the contrary, film studios are not usually so lenient financially. A Warner man to whom I talked later explained the tolerance shown Brando by saying, 'Ordinarily we wouldn't put up with it. All the demands he makes. Except – well, this picture just *had* to have a big star. Your star – that's the only thing that really counts at the box office.'

Among the company were some who felt that the social protection supplied by Brando's inner circle was preventing them from 'getting to know the guy' as well as they would have liked. Brando had been in Japan for more than a month, and during that time he had shown himself on the set as a slouchingly dignified, amiable-seeming young man who was always ready to cooperate with, and even encourage, his co-workers – the actors particularly – yet by and large was not

5

socially available, preferring, during the tedious lulls between
scenes, to sit alone reading philosophy or scribbling in a
schoolboy notebook. After the day's work, instead of accept-
ing his colleagues' invitations to join a group for drinks, a plate
of raw fish in a restaurant and a prowl through the old geisha
quarter of Kyoto, instead of contributing to the one-big-family,
house-party bonhomie that picture-making on location the-
oretically generates, he usually returned to his hotel and stayed
there. Since the most fervent of movie-star fans are the people
who themselves work in the film industry, Brando was a sub-
ject of immense interest within the ranks of the *Sayonara*
group, and the more so because his attitude of friendly remote-
ness produced, in the face of such curiosity, such wistful
frustrations. Even the film's director, Joshua Logan, was
impelled to say, after working with Brando for two weeks,
'Marlon's the most exciting person I've met since Garbo. A
genius. But I don't know what he's like. I don't know anything
about him.'

The maid had re-entered the star's room, and Murray, on
his way out, almost tripped over the train of her kimono. She
put down a bowl of ice, and with a glow, a giggle, an elation
that made her little feet, hooflike in their split-toed white
socks, lift and lower like a prancing pony's, announced, 'Appapie! Tonight on menu appapie.'

Brando groaned. 'Apple pie. That's all I need.' He stretched
out on the floor and unbuckled his belt, which dug too deeply
into the swell of his stomach. 'I'm supposed to be on a diet. But
the only things I want to eat are apple pie and stuff like that.'

Six weeks earlier, in California, Logan had told him he must trim off ten pounds for his role in *Sayonara*, and before arriving in Kyoto, he had managed to get rid of seven. Since reaching Japan, however, abetted not only by American-type apple pie but by the Japanese cuisine, with its delicious emphasis on the sweetened, the starchy, the fried, he'd regained, then doubled this poundage. Now, loosening his belt still more and thoughtfully massaging his midriff, he scanned the menu, which offered, in English, a wide choice of Western-style dishes, and after reminding himself 'I've *got* to lose weight,' he ordered soup, beefsteak with French-fried potatoes, three supplementary vegetables, a side dish of spaghetti, rolls and butter, a bottle of *sake*, salad, and cheese and crackers.

'And appapie, Marron?'

He sighed. 'With ice cream, honey.'

Though Brando is not a teetotaler, his appetite is more frugal when it comes to alcohol. While we were awaiting the dinner, which was to be served to us in the room, he supplied me with a large vodka on the rocks and poured himself the merest courtesy sip. Resuming his position on the floor, he lolled his head against a pillow, dropped his eyelids, then shut them. It was as though he'd dozed off into a disturbing dream; his eyelids twitched, and when he spoke, his voice – an unemotional voice, in a way cultivated and genteel, yet surprisingly adolescent, a voice with a probing, asking, boyish quality – seemed to come from sleepy distances.

'The last eight, nine years of my life have been a mess,' he said. 'Maybe the last two have been a little better. Less rolling in the trough of the wave. Have you ever been analysed? I was afraid of it at first. Afraid it might destroy the impulses that made me creative, an artist. A sensitive person receives fifty impressions where somebody else may only get seven. Sensitive people are so vulnerable; they're so easily brutalized and hurt just because they *are* sensitive. The more sensitive you are, the more certain you are to be brutalized, develop scabs. Never evolve. Never allow yourself to feel anything, because you always feel too much. Analysis helps. It helped me. But still, the last eight, nine years I've been pretty mixed up, a mess pretty much . . . '

The voice went on, as though speaking to hear itself, an effect Brando's speech often has, for like many persons who are intensely self-absorbed, he is something of a monologuist – a fact that he recognizes and for which he offers his own explanation. 'People around me never say anything,' he says. 'They just seem to want to hear what I have to say. That's why I do all the talking.'

Watching him now, with his eyes closed, his unlined face white under an overhead light, I felt as if the moment of my initial encounter with him were being re-created. The year of that meeting was 1947; it was a winter afternoon in New York, when I had occasion to attend a rehearsal of Tennessee Williams's *A Streetcar Named Desire*, in which Brando was to play the role of Stanley Kowalski. It was this role that first brought him general recognition, although among the New York theater's cognoscenti he had already attracted attention, through his student work with the drama coach Stella Adler and a few Broadway appearances – one in a play by Maxwell Anderson, *Truckline Café*, and another as Marchbanks opposite Katharine Cornell's Candida, in which he showed an ability that had been much praised and discussed. Elia Kazan, the director of *A Streetcar Named Desire*, said at that time, and has recently repeated, 'Marlon is just the best actor in the world.' But ten years ago, on the remembered afternoon, he was still relatively unknown; at least, I hadn't a clue to who he might be when, arriving too early at the *Streetcar* rehearsal, I found the auditorium deserted and a brawny young man stretched out atop a table on the stage under the gloomy glare of work lights, solidly asleep. Because he was wearing a white T-shirt and denim trousers, because of his squat gymnasium physique – the weight-lifter's arms, the Charles Atlas chest (though an opened *Basic Writings of Sigmund Freud* was resting on it) – I took him for a stagehand. Or did until I looked closely at his face. It was as if a stranger's head had been attached to the brawny body, as in certain counterfeit photographs. For this face was so very untough, superimposing, as it did, an almost angelic refinement and gentleness upon hard-jawed good looks: taut skin, a broad, high forehead, wide-apart eyes, an aqualine nose, full lips with a relaxed, sensual expression. Not the least suggestion of Williams's unpoetic Kowalski. It was therefore rather an experience to observe, later that after-noon, with what chameleon ease Brando acquired the character's cruel and gaudy colors, how superbly, like a guileful salamander, he slithered into the part, how his own persona

9

evaporated – just as, in this Kyoto hotel room nine years afterward, my 1947 memory of Brando receded, disappeared into
his 1956 self. And the present Brando, the one lounging there
on the *tatami* and lazily puffing filtered cigarettes as he talked
and talked, was, of course, a different person – bound to be.
His body was thicker; his forehead was higher, for his hair was
thinner; he was richer (from the producers of *Sayonara* he
could expect a salary of three hundred thousand dollars, plus
a percentage of the picture's earnings); and he'd become, as
one journalist put it, 'the Valentino of the bop generation' –
turned into such a world celebrity that when he went out in
public here in Japan, he deemed it wise to hide his face not
only by wearing dark glasses but by donning a surgeon's gauze
mask as well. (The latter bit of disguise is not so *outré* in Japan
as it may sound, since numerous Asians wear such masks, on
the theory that they prevent the spreading of germs.) Those
were some of the alterations a decade had made. There were
others. His eyes had changed. Although their *caffè-espresso*
color was the same, the shyness, any traces of real vulnerabil-
ity that they had formerly held, had left them; now he looked
at people with assurance, and with what can only be called a
pitying expression, as though he dwelt in spheres of enlight-
enment where they, to his regret, did not. (The reactions
of the people subjected to this gaze of constant commiser-
ation range from that of a young actress who avowed that
'Marlon is really a very *spiritual* person, wise and very sincere;
you can see it in his eyes' to that of a Brando acquaintance
who said, 'The way he looks at you, like he was so damn sorry

for you – doesn't it make you want to cut your throat?') Nevertheless, the subtly tender character of his face had been preserved. Or almost. For in the years between he'd had an accident that gave his face a more conventionally masculine aspect. It was just that his nose had been broken. And maneuvering a word in edgewise, I asked, 'How did you break your nose?'

'. . . by which I don't mean that I'm *always* unhappy. I remember one April I was in Sicily. A hot day, and flowers everywhere. I like flowers, the ones that smell. Gardenias. Anyway, it was April and I was in Sicily, and I went off by myself. Lay down in this field of flowers. Went to sleep. That made me happy. I was happy *then*. What? You say something?'

'I was wondering how you broke your nose.'

He rubbed his nose and grinned, as though remembering an experience as happy as the Sicilian nap. 'That was a long time ago. I did it boxing. It was when I was in *Streetcar*. We – some of the guys backstage and me – we used to go down to the boiler room in the theater and horse around, mix it up. One night I was mixing it up with this guy and – crack! So I put on my coat and walked around to the nearest hospital – it was off Broadway somewhere. My nose was really busted. They had to give me an anesthetic to set it, and put me to bed. Not that I was sorry. *Streetcar* had been running about a year and I was sick of it. But my nose healed pretty quick, and I guess I would've been back in the show practically right away if I hadn't done what I did to Irene Selznick.' His grin broadened as he mentioned Mrs Selznick, who had been the producer of the Williams play. 'There is one shrewd lady, Irene Selznick. When she wants something, she wants it. And she wanted me back in the play. But when I heard she was coming to the hospital, I went to work with bandages and iodine and mercurochrome, and – Christ! – when she walked in the door, I looked like my head had been cut off. At the least. And *sounded* as though I were dying. "Oh, Marlon," she said, "you poor, *poor* boy!" And I said, "Don't you worry about anything, Irene. I'll be back in the show tonight!" And she said, "Don't you dare! We can manage without you for – for – well, a *few* days more." "No, no," I said. "I'm okay. I want to work. Tell them I'll be back tonight." So she said, "You're in no condition, you poor darling. I *forbid* you to come to the theater." So I stayed in the hospital and had myself a ball.' (Mrs Selznick, recalling the incident recently, said, 'They didn't set his nose properly at all. Suddenly his face was quite different. Kind of tough. For months afterward I kept telling him, "But they've *ruined* your face. You must have your nose broken again and reset." Luckily for him, he didn't listen to me. Because I honestly think that broken nose made his fortune as far as the movies go. It gave him sex appeal. He was too beautiful before.')

Brando made his first trip to the Coast in 1949, when he went out there to play the leading role in *The Men*, a picture dealing with paraplegic war veterans. He was accused, at the time, of uncouth social conduct, and criticized for his black-leather-jacket taste in attire, his choice of motorcycles instead of Jaguars and his preference for obscure secretaries rather than movie starlets; moreover, Hollywood columnists studded their copy with hostile comments concerning his attitude toward the film business, which he himself summed up soon after he entered it by saying, 'The only reason I'm here is that I don't yet have the moral courage to turn down the money.' In interviews, he repeatedly stated that becoming 'simply a movie actor' was the thing furthest from his thoughts. 'I may do a picture now and then,' he said on one occasion, 'but mostly I intend to work on the stage.' However, he followed *The Men*, which was more of a *succès d'estime* than a commercial triumph, by re-creating Kowalski in the screen treatment of *A Streetcar Named Desire*, and this role, as it had done on Broadway, established him as a star. (Defined practically, a movie star is any performer who can account for a box-office profit regardless of the quality of the enterprise in which he appears; the breed is so scarce that there are fewer than ten actors today who qualify for the title. Brando is one of them; as a box-office draw, male division, he is perhaps outranked only by William Holden.) In the course of the last five years he has played a Mexican revolutionary (*Viva Zapata!*), Mark Antony (*Julius Caesar*) and a motorcycle-mad juvenile delinquent (*The Wild One*); earned an Academy Award in the role of a dockyard thug (*On the Waterfront*); impersonated Napoleon (*Désirée*); sung and danced his way through the part of an adult delinquent (*Guys and Dolls*); and taken the part of the Okinawan interpreter in *The Teahouse of the August Moon*, which, like *Sayonara*, his tenth picture, was partly shot on location in Japan. But he has never, except for a brief period in summer stock, returned to the stage. 'Why should I?' he asked with apathy when I remarked on this. 'The movies have a greater potential. They can be a factor for good. For moral development. At least some can – the kind of movies I want to do.' He paused, seemed to listen, as though his statement had been tape-recorded and he were now playing it back. Possibly the sound of it dissatisfied him; at any rate, his jaw started working, as if he were biting down on an unpleasant mouthful. He looked off into space suddenly and demanded, 'What's so hot about New York? What's so hot about working for Cheryl Crawford and Robert Whitehead?' Miss Crawford and Whitehead are two of New York's most prominent theatrical producers, neither of whom has had occasion to employ Brando. 'Anyway, what would I be in?' he continued. 'There aren't any parts for me.'

Stack them, and the playscripts offered him in any given season by hopeful Broadway managements might very well rise to a height exceeding the actor's own. Tennessee Williams wanted him for the male lead in each of his last five plays, and the most recent of these, *Orpheus Descending*, which was pending production at the time of our talk, had been written expressly as a co-starring vehicle for Brando and the Italian actress Anna Magnani. 'I can explain very easily why I didn't do *Orpheus*,' Brando said. 'There are beautiful things in it, some of Tennessee's best writing, and the Magnani part is great; she stands for something, you can understand her – and she would wipe me off the stage. The character I was supposed to play, this boy, this Val, he never takes a stand. I didn't really know what he was for or against. Well, you can't act a vacuum. And I told Tennessee. So he kept trying. He rewrote it for me, maybe a couple of times. But–' He shrugged. 'Well, I had no intention of walking out on any stage with Magnani. Not in that part. They'd have had to mop me up.' Brando mused a moment, and added, 'I think – in fact, I'm sure – Tennessee has made a fixed association between me and Kowalski. I mean, we're friends and he knows that as a person I am just the opposite of Kowalski, who was everything I'm against – totally insensitive, crude, cruel. But still, Tennessee's image of me is confused with the fact that I played that part. So I don't know if he could write for me in a different color range. The only reason I did *Guys and Dolls* was to work in a lighter color – yellow. Before that, the brightest color I'd played was red. From red down. Brown. Gray. Black.' He crumpled an empty cigarette package and bounced it in his hand like a ball. 'There aren't any parts for me on the stage. Nobody writes them. Go on. Tell me a part I could do.'

In the absence of vehicles by worthy contemporaries, might he not favor the work of older hands? Several responsible persons who appeared with him in the film had admired his reading of Mark Antony in *Julius Caesar*, and thought him equipped, provided the will was there, to essay many of the Mount Everest roles in stage literature – even, possibly, Oedipus.

Brando received reminders of this praise blankly – or, rather, he seemed to be indulging his not-listening habit. But sensing silence again, he dissolved it: 'Of course, movies *date* so quickly. I saw *Streetcar* the other day and it was already an old-fashioned picture. Still, movies do have the greatest potential. You can say important things to a lot of people. About discrimination and hatred and prejudice. I want to make pictures that explore the themes current in the world today. In terms of entertainment. That's why I've started my own independent production company.' He reached out affectionately to finger *A Burst of Vermilion*, which will be the first script filmed by Pennebaker Productions – the independent company he has formed.

And did *A Burst of Vermilion* satisfy him as a basis for the kind of lofty aims he proposed?

He mumbled something. Then he mumbled something else. Asked to speak more clearly, he said, 'It's a Western.'

He was unable to restrain a smile, which expanded into laughter. He rolled on the floor and roared. 'Christ, the only thing is, will I ever be able to look my friends in the face again?' Sobering somewhat, he said, 'Seriously, though, the first picture *has* to make money. Otherwise, there won't be another. I'm nearly broke. No, no kidding. I spent a year and two hundred thousand dollars of my own money trying to get some writer to come up with a decent script. Which used my ideas. The last one, it was so terrible I said I can do better myself. I'm going to direct it, too.'

Produced by, directed by, written by, and starring. Charlie Chaplin has managed this, and gone one better by composing his own scores. But professionals of wide experience – Orson

Welles, for one – have caved in under a lesser number of chores than Brando planned to assume. However, he had a ready answer to my suggestion that he might be loading the cart with more than the donkey could haul. 'Take producing,' he said. 'What does a producer do except cast? I know as much about casting as anyone does, and that's all producing is. Casting.' In the trade, one would be hard put to it to find anyone who concurred in this opinion. A good producer, in addition to doing the casting – that is, assembling the writer, the director, the actors, the technical crew and the other components of his team – must be a diplomat of the emotions, smoothing and soothing, and above all, must be a skilled mechanic when it comes to dollars-and-cents machinery. 'But seriously,' said Brando, now excessively sober, '*Burst isn't* just cowboys-and-Indians stuff. It's about this Mexican boy – hatred and discrimination. What happens to a community when those things exist.'

Sayonara, too, has moments when it purports to attack race prejudice, telling, as it does, the tale of an American jet pilot who falls in love with a Japanese music-hall dancer, much to the dismay of his Air Force superiors, and also to the dismay of her employers, though the latter's objection is not the racial unsuitability of her beau but simply that she has a beau at all, for she is a member of an all-girl opera company – based on a real-life counterpart, the Takarazuka Company – whose management promotes a legend that offstage its hundreds of girls lead a convent-like existence, unsullied by male presence of any creed or color. Michener's novel concludes with the lovers forlornly bidding each other *sayonara*, a word meaning farewell. In the film version, however, the word, and consequently the title, has lost significance; here the fadeout reveals the twain of East and West so closely met that they are on their way to the matrimonial bureau. At a press conference that Brando conducted upon his Tokyo arrival, he informed some sixty reporters that he had contracted to do this story because 'it strikes very precisely at prejudices that serve to limit our progress toward a peaceful world. Underneath the romance, it attacks prejudices that exist on the part of the Japanese as well as on our part,' and also he was doing the film because it would give him the 'invaluable opportunity' of working under Joshua Logan, who could teach him 'what to do and what not to do'.

But time had passed. And now Brando said, with a snort, 'Oh, *Sayonara*, I love it! This wondrous hearts-and-flowers nonsense that was supposed to be a serious picture about Japan. So what difference does it make? I'm just doing it for the money anyway. Money to put in the kick for my own company.' He pulled at his lip reflectively and snorted again. 'Back in California, I sat through twenty-two hours of script conferences. Logan said to me, "We welcome any suggestions you have, Marlon. Any changes you want to make, you just make them. If there's anything you don't like – why, rewrite it, Marlon, write it your own way." ' Brando's friends boast that he can imitate anybody after fifteen minutes' observation; to judge by the eerie excellence with which he mimicked Logan's vaguely Southern voice, his sad-eyed, beaming, aquiver-with-enthusiasm manner, they are hardly exaggerating. '*Rewrite?* Man, I rewrote the whole damn script. And now out of that they're going to use maybe eight lines.' Another snort. 'I give up. I'm going to walk through the part, and that's that. Sometimes I think nobody knows the difference anyway. For the first few days on the set, I tried to act. But then I made an experiment. In this scene, I tried to do everything wrong I could think of. Grimaced and rolled my eyes, put in all kinds of gestures and expressions that had no relation to the part I'm supposed to be playing. What did Logan say? He just said, "It's wonderful! Print it!"'

A phrase that often occurs in Brando's conversation, 'I only mean forty percent of what I say,' is probably applicable here. Logan, a stage and film director of widely recognized and munificently rewarded accomplishments (*Mister Roberts, South Pacific, Picnic*), is a man balanced on enthusiasm, as a bird is balanced on air. A creative person's need to believe in the value of what he is creating is axiomatic; Logan's belief in whatever project he is engaged in approaches euphoric faith, protecting him, as it seems designed to do, from the nibbling nuisance of self-doubt. The joy he took in everything connected with *Sayonara*, a film he had been preparing for two years, was so nearly flawless that it did not permit him to conceive that his star's enthusiasm might not equal his own. Far from it. 'Marlon,' he occasionally announced, 'says he's never been as happy with a company as he is with us.' And 'I've never worked with such an exciting, inventive actor. So pliable. He takes direction beautifully, and yet he always has something to add. He's made up this Southern accent for the part; I never would have thought of it myself, but, well, it's exactly right – it's perfection.' Nevertheless, by the night I had dinner in Brando's hotel room, Logan had begun to be aware that there was something lacking in his rapport with Brando. He attributed it to the fact that at this juncture, when most of the scenes being filmed concentrated on Japanese background (street crowds, views, spectacles) rather than actors, he had not yet worked with Brando on material that put either of them to much of a test. 'That'll come when we get back to California,' he said. 'The interior stuff, the dramatic scenes. Brando's going to be great – we'll get along fine.'

There was another reason for Logan's inability, at that point, to give his principal player the kind of attention that might have established closer harmony: he was in serious disharmony with the very Japanese elements that had contributed most to his decision to make the picture. Long infatuated with the Japanese theater, Logan had counted heavily on interlacing *Sayonara* with authentic sequences taken from the classic Kabuki theater, the masked Nō dramas, the Bunraku puppet plays; they were to be, so to say, the highbrow-lights of the film. And to this end Logan, along with William Goetz, the producer, had been in negotiation for over a year with Shochiku, the gigantic film company that controls a major part of Japan's live theatrical activities. The ruler of the Shochiku empire is a small, unsmiling eminence in his eighties, known as Mr Otani; he has a *prénom*, Takejiro, but there are few men alive on such familiar terms that they would presume to use it. The son of a butcher (and therefore, in Japan's Buddhist society, a member of the outcast group), Otani, together with a brother now dead, founded Shochiku and nurtured it to the point where, for the last four years, its payroll has been the biggest of any single company in Japan. A tycoon to rival Kok-ichi Mikimoto, the late cultured-pearl potentate, Otani casts a cloaklike shadow over the entire Japanese entertainment industry; in addition to having monopolistic control of the classic theater, he owns the country's most extensive chain of movie houses and music halls, produces many films and has a hand in radio and television. From Otani's vantage point, any transactions with the Messrs. Logan and Goetz must have looked like very small *sake*. However, he was at first in sym-pathy with their project, largely because he was impressed by the fervor of Logan's veneration for Kabuki, Nō and Bunraku, the three unquestionably genuine gems in the old man's crown, and the ones closest to his heart. (According to some specialists, these ancient arts owe their continued health mainly to his generosity.)

But Otani is not all philanthropist; when Shochiku's negotia-tions with the *Sayonara* management were supposedly concluded, the former had given the latter, for a handsome price, franchise to photograph scenes in Tokyo's famed Kabuki Theater, and, for a still handsomer honorarium, permission to make free use of the Kabuki troupe, the Nō plays and play-ers and the Bunraku puppeteers. Shochiku had also agreed to the participation of its own all-girl opera company – a necessary factor in the production of the film, since the Takarazuka troupe depicted in the novel had deeply resented Michener's 'libel' and refused any cooperation whatever. Logan, leaving for Japan, was so elated he could have flown there under his own power. 'Otani's given us carte blanche, and this is going to be it, the real thing,' he said. 'None of that fake Kabuki, that second-rate stuff, but the real thing – something that's never been put in a picture before.' And was not destined to be; for, across the wide Pacific, Logan and his associates had a personal Pearl Harbor awaiting them. Otani is seldom seen; he usually appears in the person of bland assistants, and as Logan and Goetz disembarked from their plane, a group of these informed the film-makers that Shochiku had made an error in its financial reckoning; the bill was now much higher than the initial estimate. Producer Goetz objected. Otani, certain that he held the stronger cards (after all, here were these Hollywood people in Japan, accompanied by an expensive cast, an expensive crew and expensive equipment), replied by raising the tab still more. Whereupon Goetz, himself a businessman as tough as tortoise shell, ended the negotiations and told his director they would have to make up their own Kabuki, Nō, Bunraku and all-girl opera company from among unattached, freelancing artists.

Meanwhile, the Tokyo press was publicizing the contretemps. Several papers, the *Japan Times* among them, implied that Shochiku was to be censured for having 'acted in bad faith'; others, taking a pro-Shochiku, or perhaps simply an anti-*Sayonara*, line, expressed themselves as delighted that the

Americans would not have the opportunity to 'degrade our finest artistic traditions' by representing them in a film version of 'a vulgar novel that is in no way a compliment to the Japanese people'. The papers antagonistic to the *Sayonara* project especially relished reporting the fact that Logan had cast a Mexican actor, Ricardo Montalban, in the part of a ranking Kabuki performer (Kabuki is traditionally an all-male enterprise; the grander, more difficult roles are those of women, played by female impersonators, and Montalban's assignment was to portray one such) and then had had the 'effrontery' to try and hire a genuine Kabuki star to substitute for Montalban in the dance sequences, which, one Japanese writer remarked, was much the same as 'asking Ethel Barrymore to be a stand-in'.

All in all, the local press was touchily interested in what was taking place down in Kyoto – the city, two hundred and thirty miles south of Tokyo, in which, because of its plethora of historic temples, its photogenic blue hills and misty lakes, and its carefully preserved old-Japan atmosphere, with elegant geisha quarter and paper-lantern-lighted streets, the *Sayonara* staff had decided to take most of their location shots. And, all in all, down in Kyoto the company was encountering as many difficulties as its ill-wishers could have hoped for. In particular, the Americans were finding it a problem to muster nationals willing to appear in their film – an interesting phenomenon, considering how desirous the average Japanese is of having himself photographed. True, the movie-makers had rounded up a ragbag-picking of Nō players and puppeteers not under contract to Shochiku, but they were having the devil's own time assembling a presentable all-girl opera company. (These peculiarly Japanese institutions resemble a sort of single-sex, innocent-minded Folies Bergère; oddly, few men attend their performances, the audiences being, on the whole, as all-girl as the cast.) In the hope of bridging this gap, the *Sayonara* management had distributed posters advertising a contest to select 'the one hundred most beautiful girls in Japan'. The affair, for which they expected a big turnout, was scheduled to take place at two o'clock on a Thursday afternoon in the lobby of the Kyoto Hotel. But there were no winners, because there were no contestants; none showed up.

Producer Goetz, one of the disappointed judges, resorted next, and with some success, to the expedient of luring ladies out of Kyoto's cabarets and bars. Kyoto – or, for that matter, any Japanese city – is a barfly's Valhalla. Proportionately, the number of premises purveying strong liquor is higher than in New York, and the diversity of these saloons – which range from cozy bamboo closets accommodating four customers to many-storied, neon-hued temples of fun featuring, in accordance with the Japanese aptitude for imitation, cha-cha bands and rock 'n' rollers and hillbilly quartets and *chanteuses existentialistes* and Oriental vocalists who sing Cole Porter songs with American Negro accents – is extraordinary. But however low or however deluxe the establishment may be, one thing remains the same: there is always on hand a pride of hostesses to cajole and temper the clientele. Great numbers of these sleekly coifed, smartly costumed, relentlessly festive *jolies jeunes filles* sit sipping Parfaits d'Amour (a syrupy violet-colored cocktail currently fashionable in these surroundings) while performing the duties of a poor man's geisha girl; that is, lightening the spirits, without necessarily corrupting the morals, of weary married men and tense, anxious-to-be-amused bachelors. It is not unusual to see four to a customer. But when the *Sayonara* officials began to try to corral them, they had to contend with the circumstance that nightworkers, such as they were dealing with, have no taste for the early rising that picture-making demands. To acquire their talents, and see that the ladies were on the set at the proper hour, certain of the film's personnel did everything but distribute engagement rings.

Still another annoyance for the makers of *Sayonara* involved the United States Air Force, whose cooperation was vital, but which, though it had previously promised help, now had fits of shilly-shallying, because it gravely objected to one of the basic elements of the plot – that during the Korean War some American Air Force men who married Japanese were shipped home. This, the Air Force complained, may have been the *practice*, but it was not official Pentagon policy. Given the choice of cutting out the offending premise, and thereby removing a sizable section of the script's entrails, or permitting it to remain, and thereby forfeiting Air Force aid, Logan selected surgery.

Then, there was the problem of Miss Miiko Taka, who had been cast as the Takarazuka dancer capable of arousing Air Force Officer Brando's passion. Having first tried to obtain Audrey Hepburn for the part, and found that Miss Hepburn thought not, Logan had started looking for an 'unknown', and had come up with Miss Taka, poised, pleasant, an unassuming, quietly attractive *nisei*, innocent of acting experience, who stepped out of a clerking job with a Los Angeles travel bureau into what she called 'this Cinderella fantasy'. Although her acting abilities – as well as those of another *Sayonara* principal, Red Buttons, an ex-burlesque, ex-television jokester, who, like Miss Taka, had had meager dramatic training – were apparently causing her director some concern, Logan, admirably undaunted, cheerful despite all, was heard to say, 'We'll get away with it. As much as possible, I'll just keep their faces straight and their mouths shut. Anyway, Brando, he's going to be so great *he'll* give us what we need.' But as for giving, 'I give up,' Brando repeated. 'I'm going to give up. I'm going to sit back. Enjoy Japan.'

At that moment, in the Miyako, Brando was presented with something Japanese to enjoy: an emissary of the hotel management, who, bowing and beaming and soaping his hands, came into the room saying 'Ah, Missa Marron Brando –' and was silent, tongue-tied by the awkwardness of his errand. He'd come to reclaim the 'gift' packages of candy and rice cakes that Brando had already opened and avidly sampled. 'Ah, Missa Marron Brando, it is a missake. They were meant for derivery in another room. Aporogies! Aporogies!' Laughing, Brando handed the boxes over. The eyes of the emissary, observing the plundered contents, grew grave, though his smile lingered – indeed, became fixed. Here was a predicament to challenge the rightly renowned Japanese politeness. 'Ah,' he breathed, a solution limbering his smile, 'since you rike them very much, you muss keep one box.' He handed the rice cakes back. 'And they' – apparently the rightful owner – 'can have the other. So, now everyone is preased.'

It was just as well that he left the rice cakes, for dinner was taking a long while to simmer in the kitchen. When it arrived, I was replying to some inquiries Brando had made about an acquaintance of mine, a young American disciple of Buddhism who for five years had been leading a contemplative, if not entirely unworldly, life in a settlement inside the gates of Kyoto's Nishi-Honganji Temple. The notion of a person's retiring from the world to lead a spiritual existence – an Oriental one, at that – made Brando's face become still, in a dreaming way. He listened with surprising attention to what I could tell him about the young man's present life, and was puzzled – chagrined, really – that it was not at all, or at all, a matter of withdrawal, of silence and prayer-sore knees. On the contrary, behind Nishi-Honganji's walls my Buddhist friend occupied three snug, sunny rooms brimming with books and phonograph records; along with attending to his prayers and performing the tea ceremony, he was quite capable of mixing a martini; he had two servants, and a Chevrolet in which he often conveyed himself to the local cinemas. And speaking of that, he had read that Marlon Brando was in town, and longed to meet him. Brando was little amused. The puritan streak in him, which has some width, had been touched; his conception of the truly devout could not encompass

27

anyone as *du monde* as the young man I'd described. 'It's like the other day on the set,' he said. 'We were working in a temple, and one of the monks came over and asked me for an autographed picture. Now, *what* would a monk want with my autograph? A picture of me?'

He stared questioningly at his scattered books, so many of which dealt with mystical subjects. At his first Tokyo press conference, he had told the journalists that he was glad to be back in Japan, because it gave him another chance to 'investigate the influence of Buddhism on Japanese thought, the determining cultural factor'. The reading matter on display offered proof that he was adhering to this scholarly, if somewhat obscure, program. 'What I'd like to do,' he presently said, 'I'd like to talk to someone who *knows* about these things. Because –' But the explanation was deferred until the maid, who just then skated in balancing vast platters, had set the lacquer table and we had knelt on cushions at either end of it.

'Because,' he resumed, wiping his hands on a small steamed towel, the usual preface to any meal served in Japan, 'I've seriously considered – I've very *seriously* thought about – throwing the whole thing up. This business of being a successful actor. What's the point, if it doesn't evolve into anything? All right, you're a success. At last you're *accepted*, you're welcome everywhere. But that's it, that's all there is to it, it doesn't lead anywhere. You're just sitting on a pile of candy gathering thick layers of – of *crust*.' He rubbed his chin with the towel, as though removing stale make-up. 'Too much success can ruin you as surely as too much failure.' Lowering his eyes, he looked without appetite at the food that the maid, to an accompaniment of constant giggles, was distributing on the plates. 'Of course,' he said hesitantly, as if he were slowly turning over a coin to study the side that seemed to be shinier, 'you can't *always* be a failure. Not and survive. Van Gogh! There's an example of what can happen when a person never receives any recognition. You stop relating; it puts you outside. But I guess success does that, too. You know, it took me a long time before I was aware that that's what I was – a big success. I was so absorbed in myself, my own problems, I never looked around, took account. I used to walk in New York, miles and miles, walk in the streets late at night, and never *see* anything. I was never sure about acting, whether that was what I really wanted to do; I'm still not. Then, when I was in *Streetcar*, and it had been running a couple of months, one night – dimly, dimly – I began to hear this roar. It was like I'd been asleep, and I woke up here sitting on a pile of candy.'

Before Brando achieved this sugary perch, he had known the vicissitudes of any unconnected, unfinanced, only partly educated (he has never received a high-school diploma, having been expelled before graduation from Shattuck Military Academy, in Faribault, Minnesota, an institution he refers to as 'the asylum') young man who arrives in New York from more rural parts – in his case, Libertyville, Illinois. Living alone in furnished rooms, or sharing underfurnished apartments, he had spent his first city years fluctuating between acting classes and a fly-by-night enrollment in Social Security; Best's once had him on its payroll as an elevator boy.

A friend of his, who saw a lot of him in those pre-candy days, corroborates to some extent the rather somnambulistic portrait Brando paints of himself. 'He was a brooder, all right,' the friend has said. 'He seemed to have a built-in hideaway room and was always rushing off to it to worry over himself, and gloat, too, like a miser with his gold. But it wasn't all Gloomsville. When he wanted to, he could rocket right out of himself. He had a wild, kid kind of fun thing. Once he was living in an old brownstone on Fifty-second Street, near where some of the jazz joints are. He used to go up on the roof and fill paper bags with water and throw them down at the stiffs coming out of the clubs. He had a sign on the wall of his room that said "You Ain't Livin' If You Don't Know It". Yeah, there was always something jumping in that apartment – Marlon playing the bongos, records going, people around, kids from the Actors' Studio, and a lot of down-and-outers he'd picked up. And he could be sweet. He was the least opportunistic person I've ever known. He never gave a damn about anybody who could help him; you might say he went out of his way to avoid them. Sure, part of that – the kind of people he didn't like and the kind he did, both – stemmed from his insecurities, his inferiority feelings. Very few of his friends were his equals – anybody he'd have to *compete* with, if you know what I mean. Mostly they were strays, idolizers, characters who were dependent on him one way or another. The same with the girls he took out. Plain sort of somebody's-secretary-type girls – nice enough but nothing that's going to start a stampede of competitors.' (The last-mentioned preference of Brando's was true of him as an adolescent, too, or so his grandmother has said. As she put it, 'Marlon always picked on the cross-eyed girls.')

The maid poured *sake* into thimble-sized cups, and withdrew. Connoisseurs of this palely pungent rice wine pretend they can discern variations in taste and quality in over fifty brands. But to the novice all *sake* seems to have been brewed in the same vat – a toddy, pleasant at first, cloying afterward, and not likely to echo in your head unless it is devoured by the quart, a habit many of Japan's *bons vivants* have adopted. Brando ignored the *sake* and went straight for his filet. The steak was excellent; Japanese take a just pride in the quality of their beef. The spaghetti, a dish that is very popular in Japan, was not; nor was the rest – the conglomeration of peas, potatoes, beans. Granted that the menu was a queer one, it is on the whole a mistake to order Western-style food in Japan, yet there arise those moments when one retches at the thought of more raw fish, sukiyaki, and rice with seaweed, when, however temptingly they may be prepared and however prettily presented, the unaccustomed stomach revolts at the prospect of eel broth and fried bees and pickled snake and octopus arms.

As we ate, Brando returned to the possibility of renouncing his movie-star status for the satisfactions of a life that 'led somewhere'. He decided to compromise. 'Well, when I get back to Hollywood, what I *will* do, I'll fire my secretary and move into a smaller house,' he said. He sighed with relief, as though he'd already cast off old encumbrances and entered upon the simplicities of his new situation. Embroidering on its charms, he said, 'I won't have a cook or maid. Just a cleaning woman who comes in twice a week. But' – he frowned, squinted, as if something were blurring the bliss he envisioned – 'wherever the house is, it has to have a *fence*. On account of the people with pencils. You don't know what it's like. The people with pencils. I need a fence to keep them out. I suppose there's nothing I can do about the telephone.'

'Telephone?'

'It's tapped. Mine is.'

'Tapped? Really? By whom?'

He chewed his steak, mumbled. He seemed reluctant to say, yet certain it was so. 'When I talk to my friends, we speak French. Or else a kind of bop lingo we made up.'

Suddenly, sounds came through the ceiling from the room above us – footfalls, muffled voices like the noise of water flowing through a pipe. 'Sh-h-h!' whispered Brando, listening intently, his gaze alerted upward. 'Keep your voice down. *They* can hear everything.' They, it appeared, were his fellow actor Red Buttons and Button's wife, who occupied the suite overhead. 'This place is made of paper,' he continued in tiptoe tones, and with the absorbed countenance of a child lost in a very earnest game – an expression that half explained his secretiveness, the looking-over-his-shoulder, coded-bop-for-telephones facet of his personality that occasionally causes conversation with him to assume a conspiratorial quality, as though one were discussing subversive topics in perilous political territory. Brando said nothing; I said nothing. Nor did Mr and Mrs Buttons – not anything distinguishable.

During the siege of silence, my host located a letter buried among the dinner plates, and read it while he ate, like a gentleman perusing his breakfast newspaper. Presently, remembering me, he remarked, 'From a friend of mine. He's making a documentary, the life of James Dean. He wants me to do the narration. I think I might.' He tossed the letter aside and pulled his apple pie, topped with a melting scoop of vanilla ice cream, toward him. 'Maybe not, though. I get excited about something, but it never lasts more than seven minutes. Seven minutes exactly. That's my limit. I never know why I get up in the morning.' Finishing his pie, he gazed speculatively at my portion; I passed it to him. 'But I'm really considering this Dean thing. It could be important.'

James Dean, the young motion-picture actor killed in a car accident in 1955, was promoted throughout his phosphorescent career as the all-American 'mixed-up kid,' the symbol of misunderstood hot-rodding youth with a switchblade approach to life's little problems. When he died, an expensive film in which he had starred, *Giant*, had yet to be released, and the picture's press agents, seeking to offset any ill effects that Dean's demise might have on the commercial prospects of their product, succeeded by 'glamorizing' the tragedy, and in ironic consequence, created a Dean legend of rather necrophilic appeal. Though Brando was seven years older than Dean, and professionally more secure, the two actors came to be associated in the collective movie-fan mind. Many critics reviewing Dean's first film, *East of Eden*, remarked on the wellnigh plagiaristic resemblance between his acting mannerisms and Brando's. Off-screen, too, Dean appeared to be practicing the sincerest form of flattery; like Brando, he tore around on motorcycles, played bongo drums, dressed the role of rowdy, spouted an intellectual rigmarole, cultivated a cranky, colorful newspaper personality that mingled, to a skillfully potent degree, plain bad boy and sensitive sphinx.

'No, Dean was never a friend of mine,' said Brando, in response to a question that he seemed surprised to have been asked. 'That's not why I may do the narration job. I hardly knew him. But he had an *idée fixe* about me. Whatever I did he did. He was always trying to get close to me. He used to call up.' Brando lifted an imaginary telephone, put it to his ear with a cunning, eavesdropper's smile. 'I'd listen to him talking to the answering service, asking for me, leaving messages. But I never spoke up. I never called him back. No, when I –'

The scene was interrupted by the ringing of a real telephone. 'Yeah?' he said, picking it up. 'Speaking. From where? . . . Manila? . . . Well, I don't know anybody in Manila. Tell them I'm not here. No, when I finally met Dean,' he said, hanging up, 'it was at a party. Where he was throwing himself around, acting the madman. So I spoke to him. I took him aside and asked him didn't he know he was sick? That he needed help?' The memory evoked an intensified version of Brando's familiar look of enlightened compassion. 'He listened to me. He knew he was sick. I gave him the name of an analyst, and he went. And at least his *work* improved. Toward the end, I think he was beginning to find his own way as an actor. But this glorifying of Dean is all wrong. That's why I believe the documentary could be important. To show he wasn't a hero; show what he really was – just a lost boy trying to find himself. That ought to be done, and I'd like to do it – maybe as a kind of expiation for some of my own sins. Like making *The Wild One*.' He was referring to the strange film in which he was presented as the Führer of a tribe of Fascist-like delinquents. 'But. Who knows? Seven minutes is my limit.'

From Dean the conversation turned to other actors, and I asked which ones, specifically, Brando respected. He pondered; though his lips shaped several names, he seemed to have second thoughts about pronouncing them. I suggested a few candidates – Laurence Olivier, John Gielgud, Montgomery Clift, Gérard Philipe, Jean-Louis Barrault. 'Yes,' he said, at last coming alive, 'Philipe is a good actor. So is Barrault. Christ, what a wonderful picture that was – *Les Enfants du Paradis*! Maybe the best movie ever made. You know, that's the only time I ever fell in love with an actress, somebody on the screen. I was mad about Arletty.' The Parisian star Arletty is well remembered by international audiences for the witty, womanly allure she brought to the heroine's part in Barrault's celebrated film. 'I mean, I was really in *love* with her. My first trip to Paris, the thing I did right away, I asked to meet Arletty. I went to see her as though I were going to a shrine. My ideal woman. Wow!' He slapped the table. 'Was that a mistake, was that a disillusionment! She was a tough article.'

The maid came to clear the table; *en passant*, she gave Brando's shoulder a sisterly pat, rewarding him, I took it, for the cleaned-off sparkle of his plates. He again collapsed on the floor, stuffing a pillow under his head. 'I'll tell you,' he said, 'Spencer Tracy is the kind of actor I like to watch. The way he holds back, *holds* back – then darts in to make his point, darts back. Tracy, Muni, Cary Grant. They know what they're doing. You can learn something from them.'

Brando began to weave his fingers in the air, as though hoping that gestures would describe what he could not precisely articulate. 'Acting is such a tenuous thing,' he said. 'A fragile, shy thing that a sensitive director can help lure out of you. Now, in movie-acting, the important, the *sensitive* moment comes around the third take of a scene; by then you just need a whisper from the director to crystallize it for you. Gadge' – he was using Elia Kazan's nickname – 'can usually do it. He's wonderful with actors.'

Another actor, I suppose, would have understood at once what Brando was saying, but I found him difficult to follow. 'It's what happens inside you on the third take,' he said, with a careful emphasis that did not lessen my incomprehension. One of the most memorable film scenes Brando has played occurs in the Kazan-directed *On the Waterfront*; it is the car-ride scene in which Rod Steiger, as the racketeering brother, confesses he is leading Brando into a death trap. I asked if he could use the episode as an example, and tell me how his theory of the 'sensitive moment' applied to it.

'Yes. Well, no. Well, let's see.' He puckered his eyes, made a humming noise. 'That was a seven-take scene, and I didn't like the way it was written. Lot of dissension going on there. I was fed up with the whole picture. All the location stuff was in New Jersey, and it was the dead of winter – the cold, Christ! And I was having problems at the time. Woman trouble. That scene. Let me see. There were seven takes because Rod Steiger couldn't stop crying. He's one of those actors loves to cry. We kept doing it over and over. But I can't remember just when, just how it crystallized itself for me. The first time I saw *Waterfront*, in a projection room with Gadge, I thought it was so terrible I walked out without even speaking to him.'

A month earlier, a friend of Brando's had told me, 'Marlon always turns against whatever he's working on. Some element of it. Either the script or the director or somebody in the cast. Not always because of anything very rational – just because it seems to comfort him to be dissatisfied, let off steam about something. It's part of his pattern. Take *Sayonara*. A dollar gets you ten he'll develop a hoss on it somewhere along the line. A hoss on Logan, maybe. Maybe against Japan – the whole damn country. He loves Japan *now*. But with Marlon you never know from one minute to the next.'

I was wondering whether I might mention this supposed 'pattern' to Brando, ask if he considered it a valid observation about himself. But it was as though he had anticipated the question. 'I ought to keep my mouth shut,' he said. 'Around here, around *Sayonara*, I've let a few people know the way I feel. But I don't always feel the same way two days running.'

It was ten-thirty, and Murray called on the dot.

'I went out to dinner with the girls,' he told Brando, his telephone voice so audible that I could hear it, too; it spoke above a blend of dance-band rumble and bar-room roar. Obviously he was patronizing not one of the more traditional, cat-quiet Kyoto restaurants but, rather, a place where the customers wore shoes. 'We're just finishing. How about it? You through?'

Brando looked at me thoughtfully, and I, in turn, at my coat. But he said, 'We're still yakking. Call me back in an hour.'

'Okay. Well . . . okay. Listen. Miiko's here. She wants to know did you get the flowers she sent you?'

Brando's eyes lazily rolled toward the glassed-in sun porch, where a bowl of asters was centered on a round bamboo table. 'Uh-huh. Tell her thanks very much.'

'Tell her yourself. She's right here.'

'No! Hey, wait a minute! Christ, *that's* not how you do it.' But the protest came too late. Murray had already put down the phone, and Brando, reiterating '*That's* not how you do it,' blushed and squirmed like an embarrassed boy.

The next voice to emanate from the receiver belonged to his *Sayonara* leading lady, Miss Miiko Taka. She asked about his health.

'Better, thanks. I ate the bad end of an oyster, that's all. Miiko? . . . Miiko, that was very *sweet* of you to send me the flowers. They're beautiful. I'm looking at them right now. Asters,' he continued, as though shyly venturing a line of verse, 'are my favorite flowers . . .'

I retired to the sun porch, leaving Brando and Miss Taka to conduct their conversation in stricter seclusion. Below the windows, the hotel garden, with its ultra-simple and *soigné* arrangements of rock and tree, floated in the mists that crawl off Kyoto's waterways – for it *is* a watery city, crisscrossed with shallow rivers and cascading canals, dotted with pools as still as coiled snakes and mirthful little waterfalls that sound like Japanese girls giggling. Once the imperial capital and now the country's cultural museum, such an aesthetic treasure house that American bombers let it go unmolested during the war, Kyoto is surrounded by water, too; beyond the city's containing hills, thin roads run like causeways across the reflecting silver of flooded rice fields. That evening, despite the gliding mists, the blue encircling hills were discernible against the night, for the upper air had purity; a sky was there, stars were in it, and a scrap of moon. Some portions of the town could be seen. Nearest was a neighborhood of curving roofs, the dark façades of aristocratic houses fashioned from silky wood, yet austere, northern, as secret-looking as any stone Siena palace. How brilliant they made the street lamps appear, and the doorway lanterns casting keen kimono colors – pink and orange, lemon and red. Farther away was a modern flatness – wide avenues and neon, a skyscraper of raw concrete that seemed less enduring, more perishable, than the papery dwellings stooping around it.

Brando completed his call. Approaching the sun porch, he looked at me looking at the view. He said, 'Have you been to Nara? Pretty interesting.'

I had, and yes, it was. 'Ancient, old-time Nara,' as a local cicerone unfailingly referred to it, is an hour's drive from Kyoto – a postcard town set in a show-place park. Here is the apotheosis of the Japanese genius for hypnotizing nature into unnatural behavior. The great shrine-infested park is a green salon where sheep graze, and herds of tame deer wander under trim pine trees and, like Venetian pigeons, gladly pose with honeymoon couples; where children yank the beards of unretaliating goats; where old men wearing black capes with mink collars squat on the shores of lotus-quilted lakes and, by clapping their hands, summon swarms of fish, speckled and scarlet carp, fat, thick as trout, who allow their snouts to be tickled, then gobble the crumbs that the old men sprinkle. That this serpentless Eden should strongly appeal to Brando was a bit surprising. With his liberal taste for the off-trail and not-overly-trammeled, one might have thought he would be unresponsive to so ruly, subjugated a landscape. Then, as though apropos of Nara, he said, 'Well, I'd like to be married. I want to have children.' It was not, perhaps, the *non sequitur* it seemed; the gentle safety of Nara just could, by the association of ideas, suggest marriage, a family.

'You've got to have love,' he said. 'There's no other reason for living. Men are no different from mice. They're born to perform the same function. Procreate.' ('Marlon,' to quote his friend Elia Kazan, 'is one of the gentlest people I've ever known. Possibly the gentlest.' Kazan's remark had meaning when one observed Brando in the company of children. As far as he was concerned, Japan's youngest generation – lovely, lively, cherry-cheeked kids with bow-legs and bristling bangs – was always welcome to lark around the *Sayonara* sets. He was good with the children, at ease, playful, appreciative; he seemed, indeed, their emotional contemporary, a co-conspirator. Moreover, the condoling expression, the slight look of dispensing charitable compassion, peculiar to his contemplation of some adults, was absent from his eyes when he looked at a child.)

Touching Miss Taka's floral offering, he went on, 'What other reason is there for living? Except love? That has been my main trouble. My inability to love anyone.' He turned back into the lighted room, stood there as though hunting something – a cigarette? He picked up a pack. Empty. He slapped at the pockets of trousers and jackets lying here and there. Brando's wardrobe no longer smacks of the street gang; as a dresser, he has graduated, or gone back, into an earlier style of outlaw chic, that of the prohibition sharpie – black snap-brim hats, striped suits and somber-hued George Raft shirts with pastel ties. Cigarettes were found; inhaling, he slumped on the pallet bed. Beads of sweat ringed his mouth. The electric heater hummed. The room was tropical; one could have grown orchids. Overhead, Mr and Mrs Buttons were again bumping about, but Brando appeared to have lost interest in them. He was smoking, thinking. Then, picking up the stitch of his thought, he said, 'I can't. Love anyone. I can't trust anyone enough to give myself to them. But I'm ready. I want it. And I may, I'm almost on the point, I've really got to . . .' His eyes narrowed, but his tone, far from being intense, was indifferent, dully objective, as though he were discussing some character in a play – a part he was weary of portraying yet was trapped in by contract. 'Because – well, what else is there? That's all it's all about. To love somebody.'

(At this time Brando was, of course, a bachelor, who had, upon occasion, indulged in engagements of a quasi-official character – once to an aspiring authoress and actress, by name Miss Blossom Plumb, and again, with more public attention, to Mlle. Josanne Mariani-Bérenger, a French fisherman's daughter. But in neither instance were banns ever posted. One day last month, however, in a sudden and somewhat secret ceremony at Eagle Rock, California, Brando was married to a dark, sari-swathed young minor actress who called herself Anna Kashfi. According to conflicting press reports, either she was a Darjeeling-born Buddhist of the purest Indian parentage or she was the Calcutta-born daughter of an English couple named O'Callaghan, now living in Wales. Brando has not yet done anything to clear up the mystery.)

'Anyway, I have *friends*. No. No, I don't,' he said, verbally shadow-boxing. 'Oh, sure I do,' he decided, smoothing the sweat on his upper lip. 'I have a great many friends. Some I don't hold out on. I let them know what's happening. You have to trust somebody. Well, not all the way. There's nobody I rely on to tell *me* what to do.'

I asked if that included professional advisers. For instance, it was my understanding that Brando very much depended on the guidance of Jay Kanter, a young man on the staff of the Music Corporation of America, which is the agency that represents him. 'Oh, Jay,' Brando said now. 'Jay does what I tell *him* to. I'm alone like that.'

The telephone sounded. An hour seemed to have passed, for it was Murray again. 'Yeah, still yakking,' Brando told him. 'Look, let *me* call *you* . . . Oh, in an hour or so. You be back in your room? . . . Okay.'

He hung up, and said, 'Nice guy. He wants to be a director – eventually. I was saying something, though. We were talking about friends. Do you know how I make a friend?' He leaned a little toward me, as though he had an amusing secret to impart. 'I go about it very gently. I circle around and around. I circle. Then, gradually, I come nearer. Then I reach out and touch them – ah, so gently . . .' His fingers stretched forward like insect feelers and grazed my arm. 'Then,' he said, one eye half shut, the other, à la Rasputin, mesmerically wide and shining, 'I draw back. Wait awhile. Make them wonder. At just the right moment, I move in again. Touch them. Circle.' Now his hand, broad and blunt-fingered, traveled in a rotating pattern, as though it held a rope with which he was binding an invisible presence. 'They don't know what's happening. Before they realize it, they're all entangled, involved. I have them. And suddenly, sometimes, I'm all *they* have. A lot of them, you see, are people who don't fit anywhere; they're not accepted, they've been hurt, crippled one way or another. But I want to help them, and they can focus on me; I'm the duke. Sort of the duke of my domain.'

(A past tenant on the ducal preserve, describing its seigneur and his subjects, has said, 'It's as though Marlon lived in a house where the doors are never locked. When he lived in New York, the door always *was* open. Anybody could come in, whether Marlon was there or not, and everybody did. You'd arrive and there would be ten, fifteen characters wandering around. It was strange, because nobody seemed to really know anybody else. They were just there, like people in a bus station. Some type asleep in a chair. People reading the tabs. A girl dancing by herself. Or painting her toenails. A comedian trying out his night-club act. Off in a corner, there'd be a chess game going. And drums – bang, boom, bang, boom! But there was never any drinking – nothing like that. Once in a while somebody would say, "Let's go down to the corner for an ice-cream soda." Now, in all this Marlon was the common denominator, the only connecting link. He'd move around the room drawing individuals aside and talking to them alone. If you've noticed, Marlon can't, *won't*, talk to two people simultaneously. He'll never take part in a *group* conversation. It always has to be a cozy tête-à-tête – one person at a time. Which is necessary, I suppose, if you use the same kind of charm on everyone. But even when you know that's what he's doing, it doesn't matter. Because when *your* turn comes, he makes you feel you're the only person in the room. In the world. Makes you feel that you're under his protection and that your troubles and moods concern him deeply. You have to believe it; more than anyone I've known, he radiates *sincerity*. Afterward you may ask yourself, "Is it an act?" If so, what's the point? What have you got to give him? Nothing except – and this *is* the point – affection. Affection that lends him authority over you. I sometimes think Marlon is like an orphan who later on in life tries to compensate by becoming the kindly head of a huge orphanage. But even outside this institution he wants everybody to love him.' Although there exist a score of witnesses who might well contradict the last opinion, Brando himself is credited with having once informed an interviewer, 'I can walk into a room where there are a hundred people – if there is *one* person in that room who doesn't like me, I know it and have to get out.' As a footnote, it should be added that within the clique over which Brando presides he is esteemed as an intellectual father, as well as an emotional big brother. The person who probably knows him best, the comedian Wally Cox, declares him to be 'a creative philosopher, a very deep thinker', and adds, 'He's a real liberating force for his friends.'

Brando yawned; it had got to be a quarter past one. In less than five hours he would have to be showered, shaved, break-fasted, on the set, and ready for a make-up man to paint his pale face the mulatto tint that Technicolor requires.

'Let's have another cigarette,' he said as I made a move to put on my coat.

'Don't you think you should go to sleep?'

'That just means getting up. Most mornings, I don't know why I do. I can't face it.' He looked at the telephone, as though remembering his promise to call Murray. 'Anyway, I may work later on. You want something to drink?'

Outside, the stars had darkened and it had started to drizzle, so the prospect of a nightcap was pleasing, especially if I should have to return on foot to my own hotel, which was a mile distant from the Miyako. I poured some vodka; Brando declined to join me. However, he subsequently reached for my glass, sipped from it, set it down between us, and suddenly said, in an offhand way that nonetheless conveyed feeling, 'My mother. She broke apart like a piece of porcelain.'

I had often heard friends of Brando's say, 'Marlon worshipped his mother.' But prior to 1947, and the première of *A Streetcar Named Desire*, few, perhaps none, of the young actor's circle had met either of his parents; they knew nothing of his background except what he chose to tell them. 'Marlon always gave a very colorful picture of home life back in Illinois,' one of his acquaintances told me. 'When we heard that his family were coming to New York for the opening of *Streetcar*, everybody was very curious. We didn't know what to expect. On opening night, Irene Selznick gave a big party at "21". Marlon came with his mother and father. Well, you can't imagine two more attractive people. Tall, handsome, charming as they could be. What impressed me – I think it amazed everyone – was Marlon's attitude toward them. In their presence, he wasn't the lad we knew. He was a model son. Reticent, respectful, very polite, considerate in every way.'

Born in Omaha, Nebraska, where his father was a salesman of limestone products, Brando, the family's third child and only son, was soon taken to live in Libertyville, Illinois. There the Brandos settled down in a rambling house in a countrified neighborhood; at least, there was enough country around the house to allow the Brandos to keep geese and hens and rabbits, a horse, a Great Dane, twenty-eight cats and a cow. Milking the cow was the daily chore that belonged to Bud, as Marlon was then nicknamed. Bud seems to have been an extroverted and competitive boy. Everyone who came within range of him was at once forced into some variety of contest: Who can eat fastest? Hold his breath longest? Tell the tallest tale? Bud was rebellious, too; rain or shine, he ran away from home every Sunday. But he and his two sisters, Frances and Jocelyn, were devotedly close to their mother. Many years later Stella Adler, Brando's former drama coach, described Mrs Brando, who died in 1954, as 'a very beautiful, a heavenly, lost, girlish creature'. Always, wherever she lived, Mrs Brando had played leads in the productions of local dramatic societies, and always she had longed for a more brightly footlighted world than her surroundings provided. These yearnings inspired her children. Frances took to painting; Jocelyn, who is at present a professional actress, interested herself in the theater. Bud, too, had inherited his mother's theatrical inclinations, but at seventeen he announced a wish to study for the ministry. (Then, as now, Brando searched for a belief. As one Brando disciple once summed it up, 'He needs to find something in life, something in himself, that is permanently true, and he needs to lay down his life for it. For such an intense personality, nothing less than that will do.') Talked out of his clerical ambitions, expelled from school, rejected for military service in 1942 because of a trick knee, Brando packed up and came to New York. Whereupon Bud, the plump, tow-headed, unhappy adolescent, exits, and the man-sized and very gifted Marlon emerges.

Brando has not forgotten Bud. When he speaks of the boy he was, the boy seems to inhabit him, as if time had done little to separate the man from the hurt, desiring child. 'My father was indifferent to me,' he said. 'Nothing I could do interested him, or pleased him. I've accepted that now. We're friends now. We get along.' Over the past ten years the elder Brando has supervised his son's financial affairs; in addition to Pennebaker Productions, of which Mr Brando, Sr., is an employee, they have been associated in a number of ventures, including a Nebraska grain-and-cattle ranch, in which a large percentage of the younger Brando's earnings was invested. 'But my mother was everything to me. A whole world. I tried so hard. I used to come home from school . . .' He hesitated, as though waiting for me to picture him: Bud, books under his arm, scuffling his way along an afternoon street. 'There wouldn't be anybody home. Nothing in the icebox.' More lantern slides: empty rooms, a kitchen. 'Then the telephone would ring. Somebody calling from some bar. And they'd say, "We've got a lady down here. You better come get her."' Suddenly Brando was silent. In the silence the picture faded, or, rather, became fixed: Bud at the telephone. At last the image moved again, leaped forward in time. Bud is eighteen, and: 'I thought if she loved me enough, trusted me enough, I thought, then we can be together, in New York; we'll live together and I'll take care of her. Once, later on, that really happened. She left my father and came to live with me. In New York, when I was in a play. I tried so hard. But my love wasn't enough. She couldn't care enough. She went back. And one day' – the flatness of his voice grew flatter, yet the emotional pitch ascended until one could discern, like a sound within a sound, a wounded bewilderment – 'I didn't care anymore. She was there. In a room. Holding on to me. And I let her fall. Because I couldn't take it anymore – watch her breaking apart, in front of me, like a piece of porcelain. I stepped right over her. I walked right out. I was indifferent. Since then, I've been indifferent.'

The telephone was signaling. Its racket seemed to rouse him from a daze; he stared about, as though he'd wakened in an unknown room, then smiled wryly, then whispered, 'Damn, damn, damn,' as his hand lurched toward the telephone. 'Sorry,' he told Murray. 'I was just going to call you . . . No, he's leaving now. But look, man, let's call it off tonight. It's after one. It's nearly two o'clock . . . Yeah . . . Sure thing. Tomorrow.'

Meanwhile, I'd put on my overcoat and was waiting to say good-night. He walked me to the door, where I put on my shoes. 'Well, *sayonara*,' he mockingly bade me. 'Tell them at the desk to get you a taxi.' Then, as I walked down the corridor, he called, 'And listen! Don't pay too much attention to what I say. I don't always feel the same way.'

In a sense, this was not my last sight of him that evening. Downstairs, the Miyako's lobby was deserted. There was no one at the desk, nor, outside, were there any taxis in view. Even at high noon the fancy crochet of Kyoto's streets had played me tricks; still, I set off through the marrow-chilling drizzle in what I hoped was a homeward direction. I'd never before been abroad so late in the city. It was quite a contrast to daytime, when the central parts of the town, carousel by crowds of fiesta massiveness, jangle like the inside of a *pachinko* parlor, or to early evening – Kyoto's most exotic hours, for then, like night flowers, lanterns wreathe the side streets, and resplendent geishas, with their white ceramic faces and their ballooning lacquered wigs strewn with silver bells, their hobbled wiggle-walk, hurry among the shadows toward meticulously tasteful revelries. But at two in the morning these exquisite grotesques are gone, the cabarets are shuttered; only cats remained to keep me company, and drunks and red-light ladies, the inevitable old beggar-bundles in doorways, and, briefly, a ragged street musician who followed me playing on a flute a medieval music. I had trudged far more than a mile when, at last, one of a hundred alleys led to familiar ground – the main-street district of department stores and cinemas. It was then that I saw Brando. Sixty feet tall, with a head as huge as the greatest Buddha's, there he was, in comic-paper colors, on a sign above a theater that advertised *The Teahouse of the August Moon*. Rather Buddha-like, too, was his pose, for he was depicted in a squatting position, a serene smile on a face that glistened in the rain and the light of a street lamp. A deity, yes; but more than that, really, just a young man sitting on a pile of candy.